# the male mystique

## THE PERFECT HUSBAND

*He tells you when you've got on too much lipstick,*
*And helps you with your girdle when your hips stick.*

Ogden Nash

# the male mystique

Urban G. Steinmetz

AVE MARIA PRESS
AND
TWENTY-THIRD PUBLICATIONS

"The Perfect Husband" by Ogden Nash, from *Verses From 1929 On*. Copyright, 1949, by Ogden Nash. Reprinted by permission of Little, Brown and Co.

THE MALE MYSTIQUE is a co-publishing project of Ave Maria Press, Notre Dame, Indiana 46556, and Twenty-Third Publications, Fort Wayne, Indiana 46802.

Library of Congress Catalog Card Number: 70-144042

ISBN: 0-87793-029-5

Printed in the United States of America.

# Contents

# Foreword

"Always tell the truth; you don't have to remember so much."

*R. L. Meissner*

I write this foreword to *The Male Mystique* with a good deal of satisfaction. It's a small book with very little information in it; yet a lot of my blood is scattered around on its pages. But now it is done and I can relax; it is *your* blood—you other phony males—that will be dripping over the next several chapters.

Very early in the game, I discovered that I was not talking about *other* men who like to pretend; I was talking about me. From then on, each chapter was real drudgery. There were times when I felt like John's Other Wife preparing a script for the afternoon soaps, or like a lovable, yet pregnant girl writing her "True Confession." There were many times I was tempted to say "to hell with it; why should I expose my private self to anyone?"

I suppose the answer to that is: It's about time someone did. In all of my life, I have never read an honest book about personal feelings written by a man. We always and forever try to make ourselves look better—or gloriously worse—than we are.

Neither is this book honest. But it is as honest as I can get for the moment. Just how far I am willing to go is indicated by the brevity of the chapters. Even that little look at my pretenses hurt my "masculine pride" a great deal.

So—a challenge. Are you willing to go even that far? Do you want to look at yourself from just one direction: "How much of me is genuine—and how much is phony?" If you are, then these few thoughts can be a start.

I wonder about the Male Mystique. Suppose all men did decide to become honest? Suppose we all stopped pretending; said what we thought and felt and believed and were? It would be a different world for us. How, for example, could we ever elect a president? Run a bank? Even get a job?

The thought doesn't scare me too much. I've tried as hard as most men to stop pretending, and the results have not been exactly spectacular. This generation will not see a totally honest man.

Yet we can start; improve. Raise our sons in a different way. Then maybe, someday, another generation of men will be able to relax with each other. They will know that what men say is true, and that it is genuinely they.

This book is addressed to what Father Bill McGee calls the "Phony-Baloneys"—priests, ministers, doctors, plumbers, men of every kind and description. He says that all men are phonies to a certain extent. As a somewhat phony "expert" on marriage, I couldn't agree more.

# Chapter 1
# Not Enough Loving

Maybe it's because I drink a lot, but it seems that I meet at least two different men at each party I attend. Both are dressed in the same suit.

I meet man number one early in the evening when the hostess finds that she has a "celebrity" in the crowd. (Definition of celebrity: person from out of town who has written a book.) She wants me to meet the "Important People" in her gathering (definition of Important People: people who serve on Family Betterment Committees or Youth Development Committees because it is easier than trying to cope with the old lady and kids at home) and John X is my first V.I.P.

John and I are introduced over a drink.

We chat for a while, and he tries to impress me, and I try to impress him. I casually mention that my editor is on my back to finish a manuscript for him. That is pretty big, maybe bigger than what he is doing. So he decides to level me off a little; making me smaller so he grows bigger:

"What kind of work do you do?"

"I'm Executive Director of the Family Enrichment Bureau."

"Family Enrichment Bureau. Do you sell some kind of insurance?"

"No. (Very casually.) I do a little writing and make some recordings to help people enrich their marriages."

"Yeah, I know. You mentioned that. But what do you do for a *living*?"

The second time I meet him that night, I think of him as John $X^2$. Many cocktails have magnified our friendship geometrically, and now he edges me toward a confidential corner of the room: "You said you did a little marriage counseling one time, didn't you?"

He's not that drunk, of course. Not drunk enough to be honest. So he starts out by telling me how good things are: "Good li'l cook," "wonderful mother," and then goes on: "buy her anything she needs"; and finally, two cocktails later, gets to what he wants to talk about: "There's only one li'l problem. Every time I want a li'l, she's got a headache, or she's tired, or she's got some other goddam excuse."

Sometimes it seems that every Mr. X I meet has a fine wife, lovely children; no problems. But when Mr. X gets drunk, he's never "gettin' enuf lovin'."

It's enough to make a former marriage counselor decide to drink his booze at home.

Fifteen years ago, I would have sympathized with John X, drunk or sober. I wasn't gettin' enuf lovin' at home, either. Since I am an expert on marriage, the problem, of course, was my wife. She had a hang-up. While she could occasionally be persuaded to take part in a Roman Rhythm Romp (that's something like a Heathen Romp, except we Romans always play for keeps), she always wanted something in return. That something was just plain, decent human treatment.

That's odd, isn't it? Women like to be treated like people, too.

In many respects, they *are* people. They want a little attention, a little praise, a little respect, a little genuine affection. They want a mate they can be proud of, and who is proud of them. Add a little talking, a little listening, a little honest concern, a touch of romance, and the man she is married to had better eat eggs for breakfast, dinner, and supper.

Any reasonable man would certainly want to give her the things she needs. It's just common sense. You want a tiger, you build a tiger. With the same kind of plain, decent human treatment that you expect from her.

But 20th-century man is not especially noted for his reason or his common sense in his approach to women. Behind him are many thousands of years of male mythology, built up in a time when "men were men and women were glad of it." It sounds great, yet I have a strong suspicion that our caveman ancestors drank their prototomus juice and complained to each other that they weren't getting enough at home, either.

Down through history, men have always gotten a lot more than they deserve. Instead of *being* men, and treating their women as all human beings deserve to be treated, they have been *playing* men with the confident assumption that women will drop in their arms. The game of masculinity has become more important than the reality. Let's look at some of the "rules" that all men must follow if they hope to be "real men":

A Real Man must always freely admit that he is naturally superior to woman. Didn't God create woman from a rib of Adam, and designate her as a helpmate to him? This Divine Designation puts some awesome responsibilities on man:

1.  He is automatically the Head of the Household. His wife must defer to him in all things. If she doesn't, she is trying to castrate him.

2.  He must recognize that she is only a woman, and therefore not a very deep thinker. From his eminent position, he must be extremely tolerant of her "petty concerns"—like love, and people, and communication, and personal dignity.

Real Men are strong and brave. If your wife claims to see a weakness in you, laugh at her; tell her she is wrong. Whatever you do, don't admit it, because she will then get the upper hand.

Real Men are experts on sex. If they happen to frustrate their wives a few hundred times, it is *not* because they do not know anything about sex or women; it is because their wives are "cold" or "frigid."

In other words, "Real Men" are phonies; 100 percent fakes. They are so insecure in the role they are trying to play that they don't even dare take an honest look at themselves. The game seems so important that they are willing to punish themselves through 20, 30, or even 40 years of marriage just to "be a man."

The Male Game works fairly well when we are single. Some women have been raised on male mythology, too. Now and then a woman's heart goes pitter-pat in sexual time when her big, strong Knight in Shining Armor sweeps her off her feet and drags her off to his cave. But even this woman quickly learns to like her loving practical and real. About the third time out the male animal routine gets a little tiresome, and she is liable to holler rape. This is especially true if her confident, dominant male turns out to be human. It's hard to impress wives with our virility when we are hiding from our mother-in-law in the bedroom.

All of this is written humorously. But the situation that exists in American marriage is not so funny. A huge percentage of homes have severe problems in the sexual area. Ninety percent of the middle-aged couples responding to a recent questionnaire told us that it took ten or more years for them to achieve a satisfying sexual relationship. Many never achieved it at all.

And a satisfying sexual relationship might

just be one of the most important problems facing our world today. There is no question about its importance to men; every bit of research confirms it.

But research and statistics are deceptive. The results are not always honest. Very few men are willing to report their inadequacies to anyone.

Much more valid is your own private research. When things go well at home— and this means in all areas, not just the sexual one—aren't you more confident in yourself, more tolerant of other people, generally easier to get along with? And when sex is going badly, isn't it on your mind a good deal of the time? Don't you tend to be irritable, indecisive, intolerant? Honest, now.

If it is true that sex *is* that important to you, doesn't it make sense to make it a permanent, loving relationship instead of a sometimes thing?

It seems to me that every married man has a choice to make:

1. He can keep on playing "Real Man." If he does, he will build a woman who is frigid and cold, and a life for himself that is never satisfying.

2. He can begin to face up to himself as a person, not as a myth. When he does, it

will hurt. But he will begin to see other people respond to him.

But separating man from myth is not easy. The greatest myth of all blocks our way; one that says, "Men are blunt, direct, honest. Only women are devious." If we are silly enough to believe that one, it will take us more than a lifetime to separate fact from fiction.

But if we start out by admitting that we *may* be phonies, the search should be worthwhile. Will you make it with me? As I put down my thoughts on paper, I will be looking, too—at me. Perhaps when we've finished, we will not be Real Men any longer. But we can be real genuine people.

Perhaps I am a dreamer, but I would like to see a world with the figures on sex reversed. In this New World, 90 percent of the men would be "gettin' enuf lovin' " at home—and giving enough love to make their women comfortable, confident, feminine. I don't see too many problems in a world of this kind, because no one has any particular need to step on people and "prove" himself.

And this world is achievable if enough men get *plain damn selfish*. You want a tiger, you build yourself a tiger. With decent, human, *Christian* treatment.

# Chapter 2
# Too Much Loving

Sometimes I long for the Good Old Days.

In those days, sexual counseling was a snap. Nearly every case was alike. Symptoms: Woman wan and drawn, physically exhausted. Problem: Insists she is married to sex fiend. Chased around the bed all night. Man: anxious and depressed, married to cold potato. Solution: Convince woman that husband is just Red-Blooded American Boy. "Slow down a little, Suzy; let him catch you more often." "John, give her more nonsexual love; then she will want to love you." Man slows down; woman speeds up; case solved; counselor is hero.

But today the person who goes to bed

with track shoes on is just as liable to be the man. Times have changed dramatically, and today a few hundred thousand people and articles have told the New Woman: "It's all right if you do this thing. As a matter of fact, it should be a lot of fun. It's love, baby, and love is what you need. Go get it."

Sound like a male dream of married heaven? You bet.

Except that poor old pappy hasn't quite caught up with the times. He is still playing Real Man—and Real Men are always the aggressors. We are married to Tender Flowers—and we must decide when they will bloom. Our delicate little egos will not permit our wives to play the "masculine" me. So we sulk—and many men who find themselves with sexually aggressive wives become impotent and afraid and unsure of themselves.

Isn't it time we stop this nonsense?

As a matter of fact, something pretty wonderful is starting to happen in this married world of ours. Suddenly, both men and women have the opportunity of becoming sexually free; to love and enjoy as God intended them to love and enjoy. Today's woman doesn't have a "duty" to perform; she has a husband to love. And today's husband doesn't have a "helpmate" to "give him enough to keep him from running around"; he has a wife to complete him, to make him a whole person.

Why is it so hard for men to relax and enjoy this new idea of married sexual love? Why can't we face each other as people—two people who are in love? Why do we become threatened and upset when our wives turn out to be people, too, with sexual needs of their own?

Perhaps the sexual revolution has all happened too fast. The man simply hasn't had time to adjust to it. He is still plagued with all kinds of hangovers from the "good old days."

Frankly, most men are afraid of women who are free; all through history we have kept them "in their place." Women were second-class citizens, and they knew it—and acted like it. Because no human being can really develop and grow in a condition of virtual slavery, a big percentage of women were little and petty and resentful and bitchy and masochistic. They took pride in their "self-sacrifice"—and punished their husbands and children with it every day. Their husbands were tense and frustrated and insecure in their masculinity—and constantly tried to prove themselves by stepping on other people. So eventually we managed to create a world that was little and petty and phony and distrustful because that is the kind of people we create in homes that are half slave and half free.

It doesn't make sense. Yet most men are still not willing to take a chance and permit their wives to be free. In some unreasonable way we believe that if "we give these women an inch, they will take a mile." Somehow, they will take over. Isn't that what is happening today? Don't we have a female-dominated society?

Come on, fellows, it's honesty we're talking about. Just *what* part of society does woman dominate?

Is it the Church? There she sits on a pedestal: the "heart of the home," who is somehow supposed to create love—while running around pregnant most of the time. Her place? It is an "honored" place. She is a "good" nun—without power or authority to run her own affairs or even choose her own clothes. She is a "beloved" wife; with the privilege of loving, honoring, and *obeying*. She is treated like a kid.

Does she dominate politics? Statesmanship? Schools? Business? Industry? Advertising? Just where is this dominating woman?

The only reasonable place where the

woman might be dominant is in the home. At least it's a safe place for men to point; you can't count noses there.

But even in the home, we have to ask the honest question: Does mom *want* to dominate the home? Or is she forced into that position?

Some years ago, I conducted an informal survey in my office on the question of authority in the home. I asked more than 200 women the question, "Who do you think should be the head of the household?" Then I kept track of the results.

*Not one* of these women wanted to be boss. Quite a few wanted to share authority. Most wanted the final responsibility to be the man's.

Yet *at least half* of the women queried could be described as "dominating women." They actually *were* "head of the household." Why—when they said they did not want to be?

Knowing the men in these households led me to a conclusion: The women took charge because they had to. Decisions weren't being made, so the woman made them. Nearly all made them reluctantly. And they were very uncomfortable when they did so.

Were these women so different from

men? Suppose we selected 200 men who worked in a particular place and asked them the question, "Would you like to be boss of your organization?"

Unless I am badly mistaken, a very large percentage would answer, "No, I would not want the final responsibility." Quite a few would like to share the authority. *But not with women.* When it comes to the household, men insist on being boss, *even though they have neither the competence nor the inclination to be head of anything.* Most men, I believe, want to be acknowledged as boss of the home, but then refuse to assume responsibility for that home.

What happens in any organization when the big chief says, "I make the decisions, but you get the blame if something goes wrong"? The same thing happens in a home. When the chief turns out to be nothing but a big wind, the Indians rebel.

Women are rebelling all over the country. Some of their rebellion is not pretty. We see thousands of women who have completely discarded any sense of basic responsibility or personal integrity. They slowly starve their families on TV dinners, packaged cakes, and instant breakfasts. They show their families their immature hostility by becoming completely involved in church work, youth work, family betterment committees, bridge clubs, bazaars; and when they do, they get petty and small. No woman likes herself when she is discarding her basic responsibilities.

Just whose fault is this silly feminine rebellion? Certainly the woman herself has to assume a large share of the blame. There are many ways in which she can express herself; there is no need to do so by losing her sense of dignity and integrity.

Yet a thinking man should at least be able to sympathize with her rebellion. As a matter of fact, if we claim we are chiefs—and most of us claim to be chiefs—then this is *Our Indian* that is acting irresponsibly. There's another thought, too; if *she* were the chief, and acted as we have acted, we probably would have burned the village a long time ago.

But most modern women are not that immature in their rebellion. They don't try to put a man down; they only try to lift themselves up; to demand that they be treated as persons. Like men, they know they have to be able to look at themselves and like what they see.

One of the loveliest forms of this kind of rebellion is sexual aggression. The woman looks at herself and says, "I am a sexual person, with sexual needs, and I'm glad of it. I refuse to pretend any longer. Recognize me for what I am."

Where is the threat to the male ego? Isn't that the kind of response we are all looking for? Why must we always be the arrow and she the target? Why not let her be, and then relax and enjoy what she is?

Thousands of couples have discovered what sex can be like when it is no longer a proving ground for the male ego. Millions more can do so—if the men will permit it. Mature sexual intercourse is a free and loving act between two free and loving people. Anything less is degrading.

# Chapter 3
# The Things Men Do to Themselves

"Real Men" sure like to hurt themselves.

John $X^2$ was a Real Man. After many months of boxing around (he made a donation to social services, checked me out over coffee a number of times, invited me to speak at Rotary) we finally sat down as "friend to friend" in the counseling office. During the next few months a tale of terrible self-destruction slowly emerged. Even then, he couldn't tell it himself. Instead, he begged and pleaded and nagged, until finally his wife came in and told it for him.

Sally X was a beautiful woman but a very hostile one at that first interview. She let me know immediately that she was here only as a favor to Father Y, who had urged her to give John "one more chance." John, she said, was impossible; she detested him. What she really wanted was a divorce.

Even Sally wasn't about to tell me why. She kept opening the door and then closing it again. She'd start each statement with "he's not a man" but then would tell me about how he "is always hollering at the kids" or "bragging about himself." It took her a long time to admit that "he is not a man, to *me*." Because Sally was a woman, and her integrity was at stake, too. "Maybe John was right. Maybe he is not a man— because I am not a woman."

Their "love life" emerged as a tragic comedy of misinformation and pretense. The last few months of their courtship had been an exciting and terrifying time of guilt, fear, wanting, and compromise. They could not touch each other; this they knew with certainty. Touching was spelled with a capital Sin. Yet they could not *not* touch each other, either; they were young, and in love, and passionate, and overwhelmingly curious.

Their "honeymoon" was pathetic. All day long he sweated through the reception, and that night their "consummation" was over before it really began. So he must try, again and again, because he is a "Real Man," and all men can satisfy their wives. By morning he feels like a failure and by morning she knows that what mother had often hinted at—that all men are animals—is certainly true.

The next ten years were an endless repetition of their honeymoon. John would leave the bed in the morning angry, frustrated, upset; wondering what was wrong with him. He would think about sex, and secretly read books by "noted authorities," and would leave them around for Sally to read—and come back to bed and frustrate her again. Sometimes, perhaps when they had both had a drink or two, it would start a little better, because John *did* love Sally, and when he was drinking, he was a little more honest. He could tell her he loved her then; tell her he wanted and needed to please her. But the ending was always the same; he would ejaculate too soon. Then he would turn his back and hate himself, and Sally would look at that seemingly satisfied and resting back and hate him, too. Once he swore at her and, once, in utter disgust, she told him: "You're not a man; you're a rabbit."

John's final humiliation came one night

when he was ready to begin the sex act, and the penis refused to stand erect. In one brief moment, his doubts of himself moved to certainty; he was a failure.

Impotent! This is something that never happens to Real Men. Real Men are sexually aggressive. They are always instantly ready. They are as phony as a three-dollar bill.

It would be nice to believe that we were talking about John, Extreme Case; the type we see in marriage counseling. A sick guy. All the rest of us Real Men don't have those kinds of problems. We are not too fast for our wives, we don't frustrate them. We don't worry about our sexual performance. It is always at least adequate; sometimes it is excellent.

Except for those of us who are striving for honesty.

Honesty. A tough word; one we would rather talk about than practice. One that we hide under a whole bundle of male myths and male pride.

Honesty. A word that I would like you to think about—but which I shy away from myself.

As I write this word and let it burn into me again, I find I am going to do something that I never intended to do when I started this book. I am going to try to be honest with you, the people who are making the search for manliness with me.

John $X^2$—sexually insecure, inadequate, sometimes even impotent—is the Urb Steinmetz of 15 years ago. It is a painful chapter that I write here, because I can remember all too well the pain I inflicted on an undeserving Jeanette, and I am ashamed of it. But mostly, I suppose, I remember the pain inflicted on me; the hundreds, perhaps thousands of hours that I spent detesting myself, wondering if I were a man.

Moreover, some of John $X^2$ remains in me today—Urb Steinmetz, former marriage counselor, family life "authority"—whatever that might mean. There are times— sometimes weeks at a time—when I ejaculate too soon. There are times— sometimes weeks at a time—when I have difficulty in sustaining an erection.

I suppose it is easier for me to say this because I know, now, that I am not alone. Over the years, I have been fortunate enough to listen to thousands of couples, and have come to realize that sexual intercourse is not an isolated act; instead, everything that we have been and done through a lifetime of living "makes love" with us every time we love. I finally know, now, that sexual intercourse is not just something that we do; sexual intercourse is what we are. And I know, too, that none of us are all that good.

I know, now, that every man has days when he feels like a loser, and when he goes to bed at night he acts like a loser. The human being cannot be separated into arms, and legs, and brains, and penises, with each of them acting separately. On those rare days when we feel strong, and confident, and considerate, and loving, the penis will be strong, and confident, and considerate, and loving. But these are the perfect days. How many of them have you had lately?

Every man has days, and weeks, and even years when the penis ejaculates sooner than he would like it to; or when it is not as firm as he would wish it to be. And I think it is about time that someone said so.

It makes no sense to have millions of men sitting in terrible isolation and loneliness and feeling like failures. It makes even less sense for men to spend their hard-earned bucks on sex manuals, "male" magazines and movies, trying to discover some wondrous technique that will send their women into instant ecstasy. And the most nonsensical of all are the millions of men who are so insecure that they are constantly looking for another woman who will help them "prove" their masculinity.

These are the prices we pay for believing our own mythology about "Real Men." Real Men can do this thing. Real Men satisfy their wives. And Real Men have to prove that they can, or they are not men at all.

Someday in the not too distant future, we will discard the mythology of Real Men. Both men and women will begin to "Tell it like it is," and then we can relax and love each other. It will be a real world, and that is the only kind that people can live in.

In it men and women will come to recognize that there are no Real Men; just people. And male people have a few *man* days, quite a few *little boy* days, and even a few *infant* days.

On that beautiful future day, men will still have bosses who drive them crazy, children they don't understand, and bank balances that look like a communist flag. So sometimes they will bring to bed with them penises that are very uncertain, and will ejaculate too soon. On the really bad days, they may not be able to have an erection at all.

But neither the man nor the woman will worry about it. They will not expect Mr. Supermale to create "The Great Orgasm in the Sky." He won't be expected to "send" her; just to love her.

Thousands of happy couples have already entered the future. They have discarded the notion that their bed is a proving ground for the male ego. Instead, it has become a very special place where they build each other up, reassure each other, strengthen each other, love each other.

It's a great bed to be in. But Real Men will never get there.

# Chapter 4
# The Things Men Do to Their Women

Just this morning, I received my first Jesus letter. A nice—and very perceptive—person wrote in and compared the work we are doing here with the Work of the Lord. I was wondering when someone would notice.

But a very bad thing happened. The Pharisees in our office, Betty Schmidt and Chuck Tooman, happened to get hold of the letter and showed it to my wife, Jeanette. Now the three of them are gleefully fashioning a crown of thorns, and have decided that I probably *could* walk on the water—but only because of the size of my feet.

Actually, Jesus has been a bothersome person for a Catholic marriage counselor.

During my early years, I felt strongly that he didn't quite understand how married relationships worked.

There was this story about the adulteress, for example. Everybody who is anybody knows that female adultery is the ultimate threat to the male ego, and that it simply can't be tolerated. So here was this group of sound, solid, substantial Real Men who had the only practical solution for a vicious woman; they were going to rock her to sleep—with rocks.

But then Christ stepped in. A do-gooder; an impractical dreamer. He kneels and writes something in the sand. Stalling for time, no doubt. Putting on a big show; distracting the guys' attention. Then he looks at the Real Men and says, "Let him who is without sin throw the first stone." A kind of shoddy, illogical trick. What did their sins have to do with the facts? This woman was an adulteress; she was caught at it. Yet the trick worked; the men walked away.

Then he makes matters worse by telling her that since there is no one left to condemn her, he is not going to condemn her either. He set a very bad precedent there; you can't go around encouraging adultery in women.

The trouble with Christ is that he

listened to people. No doubt she explained to him her silly, feminine reasons for her behavior, and he was unduly influenced by them. Somehow she must have persuaded a gullible Jesus that what she had done was not entirely her fault.

Perhaps she told him a story something like the one that a hundred adulteresses have told me in marriage counseling. A story that began on her wedding day, or shortly after, or maybe even a long time before. A story of what it is like for a loving, responsive woman to live with a Real Man.

Perhaps she told Christ that she married her man because she loved him, and needed to be loved in return, and know that she would be loved. And then discovered that he was much more concerned about himself, and especially about his "masculinity," than he was about love, and her.

Perhaps Sally told him how John immediately started to destroy her, making her feel little so he could feel big. How he began on their "honeymoon" to compare her with his mother, and his sisters and, even, when he was angry, with an old girl-friend or two. Maybe Christ heard about the thousands of times John "helped" her, by telling her how to cook his meals, and how to wash clothes, and even how to nurse the baby.

John's sarcasm, too, was probably a part of the conversation between Christ and Sally. She was "just like her old lady." She walked like a farmer; her household was completely disorganized. Once a day he asked her, "Can't you ever do anything right?" and now and then suggested, "If you don't have anything constructive to say, keep your big mouth shut!"

And then there were his demands. The demands that she live a loveless day and become a lover at bedtime. Reminders of her "duty" as a wife.

And sometimes the begging and the pleading and the "Oh, poor me," times when she looked at him in utter disgust and looked at herself in the same way for giving in to this worm.

Maybe Sally told Christ, as a hundred Sallys have told me, "When I woke up in the morning, I looked on the dresser to see if he had left his two pieces of silver there. Because that's how it feels to 'make love'— without love."

And maybe Sally told Christ what this did to her as a person. How she felt unloved and unlovable, and how she couldn't stand to be that way. So she slowly built herself a little dreamworld of love, and lived in it whenever she could. How she tried, through a kind of vicarious osmosis, to absorb a little love from the first-century equivalents of soap operas and romance magazines.

And how she slowly built a dream-man to hold her and love her while John was hurting her and criticizing her. And how that dream-man grew larger and larger as John made her feel smaller and smaller. And how that dream-man walked in one day to deliver her goat's milk and she didn't even know he was a dream, but thought he was real. And how he swept her off feet that were already tottering, and when it was over she didn't see two pieces of silver on the table, but thought it was love there.

Christ may have listened to this silly, feminine tale. But how did he persuade sound, practical, Real Men to accept it?

What did he write in the sand? Many people feel that he wrote the sins of the men who would do the stoning. But this doesn't fit the character of the persistent do-gooder who demands that everyone become better than they are. He wouldn't just hurt them; instead, he would help them look at themselves and realize they had things of their own that needed doing;

things that were far more important than stoning a woman.

Perhaps he drew a separate picture for each man present. Perhaps he showed this man his own home and what he was doing to help create a potential adulteress. And perhaps, as people do, each man went home thoughtfully, and some grew up; some forgot the picture, and some said, "To hell with it; I will love her when she loves me."

But why didn't Christ throw rocks at the Real Men? That's what I generally do, because I am a product of my generation. I am thoroughly imbued with the concept of Real Men; and Real Men are "naturally" superior to women. Therefore, if there is trouble in the home, it *must* be the man's fault. Punish him if he doesn't correct it.

But maybe Christ let those Real Men walk away unscathed because he is a Grownup and he understood them. Perhaps he knew that Sally's John was neither deliberately mean nor deliberately arrogant; he was just stupid. He was trained to believe that you "love" women by conquering them, and he tried to be faithful to his belief.

Perhaps Christ even understood Sally's dream-man. Not necessarily a "despoiler of women"; not as uncomplicated as "taking what he can get wherever he can get it." But instead, a very ordinary man who is a lot like Sally; a person who has lived without love, yet who needs love.

Perhaps Sally and John walked away from Christ hand in hand. But before they did, he helped her to understand that every man wants to be a dream-man, especially to his own wife. That a woman, too, has to grow up, and to look at her man and see through his pettiness and his pickiness and even his abuse to the frightened little boy underneath who needs constant reassurance before he can become a man—a *real* man.

# Chapter 5
# The Charging Linebacker

Writing this book is ruining a good man. Nearly every Sunday afternoon for the last ten years or so, I have sat in front of the TV, watching with pure joy as Ray Nitschke stepped on linemen and creamed quarterbacks. Ray was my ideal. Ray had conquered fear.

Now I sit in front of the same set and ask myself a lot of silly questions. Why do I enjoy seeing one man trampling another? Is this, perhaps, what I would like to do? And how about this fear? Has Ray really conquered it? Or is he trying to prove his "manliness" to himself by conquering others every Sunday afternoon? Is it courage that drives him, or is it fear? Fear of himself?

I cannot answer the question for Ray Nitschke, of course. But Urb Steinmetz is becoming uncomfortably aware that he does a lot of silly things because of fear. Fear that someone will discover that I am not a Real Man; that I am afraid.

And I *am* afraid. Afraid of hundreds of things. Afraid of the young, strong, aggressive men who occasionally challenge me; men who have not yet drunk too much beer and sat behind too many desks and whose stomachs are flat and hard where my potbelly rides. Afraid of my kids; I may not have raised them right. Maybe they don't love me enough; maybe they will leave me if I tell them how I honestly feel. Afraid to drop in on old friends; they may not want to see me on that day. Besides, they haven't dropped in on *me* in a long time, which is certainly an indication that they don't like me anymore. Afraid of Jeanette, and my love for her; I might fail her sexually, and then, perhaps, she will leave me. Afraid to meet my old dentist on the street, because I have recently changed dentists, and he may ask me why. Reluctant to go to hunting camp this year, because I have worn out my need for three unending days of poker and booze, but afraid to tell my old friends that I do not want to go—afraid even to go and play cards when I feel like it and drink when I feel like it—they may think I'm getting too good for them. And above all, I'm afraid to lose good friends, because I don't have too many of them and they are precious to me.

Yet, my problem is not fear. Fear is something we all have. It's just another of those components of masculinity that we need to face and learn to live with. It can be a good thing, a healthy thing, if we recognize it and admit its existence to ourselves. But when we hide it, cover it up, pretend that it doesn't exist, we tear ourselves apart. It's hard enough to live a mature life when we are constantly battling other people. It's impossible when we battle ourselves and pretend that an important part of us doesn't exist.

And a lot of men do live their entire lives pretending that they are not afraid of anything. I'm sure that you know a few. You may want to think of them now as we continue together our search for the real meaning of masculinity:

There is the man who has very little self-confidence. He is afraid to show people that he likes them; they might not like him in return. He covers it up by being hostile and aggressive, and keeps repeating, "I don't give a damn what people think of me." He starts off each new relationship by insulting people, criticizing them, putting them down. Without even knowing it, he is saying, "I can't afford to take a chance. I will let people see the worst part of me. Then, if they like me in spite of myself, I will show them I like them."

You all know this man. He is a very lonely person, and he doesn't need to be. All that he has to do is to face his fear of being unloved and learn to laugh at it. All of us want to be liked; all of us have many qualities that other people like. All of us are lonely at times. But if we want people to like us, we need to be likable people.

We all know another kind of man who is tremendously afraid of his sexual prowess. We can meet him in the bar tonight—or in the cocktail lounge. He will be sitting on the corner stool and telling the bartender about all the women he is keeping happy, and will be trying to put the make on every unattached female who enters the place. He will not face the fact that he has a hundred sexual hang-ups. Instead, he must constantly pretend—even to himself—that he is a Real Man.

All that he has to do is go home and say to his wife, "I've been a fool, honey; I don't know all of the answers to this thing; let's see if we can work them out together." But this means facing his fears, and this he will not do.

Then there is your neighbor who owes everybody in town. He continues to buy and buy; he has a new car, new snow machine, new carpeting. Yet his wife is an excellent manager.

Why does he continue to buy? He is afraid of his neighbors, afraid that they will recognize him as a financial failure. But most of all, he is afraid of himself; he has to "prove" to himself that he is a man who can do as well as anyone else.

And why doesn't he turn financial matters over to his capable wife? That would be really facing his fear: "I am financially irresponsible. I need help." Not an easy job for any of us to do.

We have all been brought up in a phony little world that says, "Men are not afraid of anything." During our growing-up years, our parents, teachers, and friends have told us so in hundreds of different ways, until finally it becomes a part of our male "religion": If you're afraid of something, don't admit it. Do something that proves you're not.

And that is stupid.

My own fears are becoming much easier to live with as I finally begin to face them and admit them. As I slowly and reluctantly drag them out into the light, I find that I can handle them.

How about that young, strong, aggressive man? He's tougher than I am. But I've lived a little longer, have more experience. It could just be an even match. My kids? It's certain that I haven't raised them right; no one ever does. But it's never too late to start some real communications, and when I do, I'm going to have a little more confidence in myself . . . a little more confidence in them. My wife? I've failed her many times before, and she hasn't left me yet. She loves me; and she's going to love me a lot more if I face my sexual fears and talk them over with her. My friends? They are going to be glad I dropped in because they, too, have been afraid to make the first move.

Fears that are faced are fears that can be handled. And yet I know there are many more that I haven't even recognized yet. It took half a lifetime to learn that "Real Men are not afraid, and if they are, they don't admit it." It's going to take the other half to admit that men *are* afraid, and to find my fears, and to start to handle them in a reasonable way. Yet with each one discovered, admitted, and handled comes a little more confidence, a little more honesty, and perhaps, even a little more maturity.

Perhaps, in a way, we're all charging linebackers, going through life with our fears hidden behind us; never in front of us where we can look at them. What are *you* afraid of? What do you do to hide your fears? Does it make any sense?

# Chapter 6
# The Game of Let's Pretend

Today I have conquered smoking again.
Since 9:05 I haven't had a single coughing,
cancer-forming cigarette, and it is almost
ten o'clock. It could be another day of many
victories. It's starting out like Tuesday. I
quit smoking three times that day, and all
without a moment's regret.

But Tuesday was great for another
reason. On that day I almost stopped
thinking. It was a relaxed and comfortable
and lazy time in which I solved many of the
problems of humanity. I wrote a nasty
letter to a pastor informing him that he was
nasty. I straightened out one of the kids who
brought home an E that was not excellent.

And not once, during all of that day, did I permit myself to confront Urb Steinmetz, Real Man. All of my effort was directed toward "loving others."

I would like to make this another day like Tuesday. But on the desk in front of me, the paper thunderstorm is starting to gather. There is a note from the editor that says, "Urb, baby, we like to have it on time." There is a note from my secretary that says, "Please observe note from Editor." And finally, there is Chapter 1 of *The Male Mystique*, which brashly says, "I am going to try to be honest with you. Let's make the search for the meaning of manhood together."

So—back to the slaughterhouse. Just which artery are we strong enough—and masochistic enough—to open today?

Perhaps we should take one last look at honesty before we move on to a better definition of masculinity. Let's look again at our favorite masculine game—the game of "Let's Pretend." But let's start with the other guy . . . we all do so much better when we're looking at someone else.

Let's start with the clergy, those super-human types who stand in front of us on Sunday and inspire us with their talks on virtue. And let's be a little more charitable than we usually are when we gossip about the clergy. They are not liars; just men. Phony men. Raised in a Real Man's world.

Like all men, clergymen try to be honest in a dishonest sort of way. They have been trained to believe that all men need an example, someone to look up to. As priests and ministers, they have to *be* that example. But that doesn't fit very well with that very ordinary human being who stands before us on Sunday. The one who is afflicted with colds, gall bladder, hemorrhoids, hang-ups on women, an impossible housekeeper, and seven meetings a week with the "pillars of the church." That man *knows* he is human. But he sincerely believes that it is not good for *us* to know.

So, in typical male "honesty," Father pretends. He stands up there in all his glory on Sunday morning, and just to look at him, we *know* he must be holier than we are. He's dressed in holiness; surrounded by holiness. And the sermon that he gives us— perhaps on honesty—is beautiful. He subtly lets us know that honesty is possible for everyone, with the help of God's grace. By forgetting to mention his own struggle with honesty, he lets us feel that *he* has achieved it.

But maybe there is one minor problem

with Father's sermon. Do you listen to it? Do you listen to anyone who pretends that he has no problems with honesty? Or do you think that he is so far above the battle (or, if you know him personally, so dishonest) that there is no use talking to him?

"But Father is 'different.' He has to pretend. I'm a doctor."

Yes. You're a doctor. So you tell your patients honestly:

"I don't know what the hell is wrong with you, Joe. But I'll give you a shot of penicillin and a prescription for tranquilizers. That clears up almost everything."

"Here. Take these green pills. They're just expensive aspirins, but I think your problem is all in your head anyway."

You're talking to the PTA. Subject: the medical profession. You say, "About half of all medical education is a complete waste of time."

Doctors are straightforward, blunt, honest.

Businessmen? They never pretend. Ask any banker who is working with them on a loan—

And bankers. And politicians. And the "ordinary working stiff" who is talking about his job . . .

But let's get a little closer to home.

Husbands, do you sometimes pretend? Maybe, even in your honest life, there was a time when:

You let your wife know that you knew everything about raising children.

About ten o'clock at night you had a brilliant thought, and told your wife (who was in sweat shirt and curlers), "Gee you look cute tonight, honey."

You gave her the impression that the place where you work is largely run by males and a few ancient females—

You somehow implied: "My mother is a saint and I love her dearly."

You suggested: "Can't you be reasonable?" (Like I am?)

And, of course, fathers are always honest:

"D in arithmetic? Why, when I was a kid . . ."

"Yes, I played a little in high school. One day the coach said to me, 'Get in there, Joe, and . . .' " (Give all the players a drink?)

"Dammit, *boys* don't cry." (Look at me; I never did.)

"We'd better take some of these beer bottles out tonight, Jane; when the kids get up in the morning . . ."

"I love every one of you just alike . . ."

Good old honest Dad. The problem is

not *if* he pretends. It is when, and how much. Want to look at yourself? Honestly?

If we want to, we can all make a pretty good case for pretending. The priest: "If my parishioners ever knew what I was really like, they'd lose all confidence in the Church."

The doctor: "If my patients ever find out how unsure of myself I really am, I won't be able to help them."

Husbands: "Every woman needs a man who is strong and decisive. What happens if she discovers . . . ?"

And Dad: "I want my son to be better than I was. If he ever did the things that I did when I was his age, I think I'd kill him."

So—we pretend. Pretend because we have been taught to pretend. We've been brought up in a phony world. Sometimes even, we pretend because we think it is the best thing to do. We want to give a "good example," even if that example is false.

The trouble is Aunt Jane. We all have an Aunt Jane. She is the one who drops in at two o'clock on Sunday afternoon when the kids are home. She is half in the bag and proceeds to tell all: "Remember, John, when you and that Aldercot boy . . ."

Even clergymen have Aunt Janes; lots of them. They are the pillars who say, "Yes,

Father. We agree. You are certainly right, Father. Yes, yes, yes." And then they go out and tell the parishioners about how the pastor and the assistant hate each other . . .

And doctors: Wow! "All she had was a wart on her tail and he removed her whole . . ."

In other words, does it do much good to pretend? Can we get away with it? Sometimes I think that kids don't rebel when they hit their teens; they just get wise to us.

But there is another, much more important reason for constantly looking at ourselves and our pretensions. How does it feels to be a phony? How much do you like yourself?

I doubt if any male of this generation can ever completely stop pretending. But I think it would take a lot less booze, tranquilizers, and head-shrinkers to keep us going if we tried a little harder.

# Chapter 7
# Busytell

It is eleven o'clock on a Friday morning and something is missing to make my week complete. Joe is what's missing. Joe works for the State of Michigan, but that is not his primary occupation. His primary occupation is Busytell.

Joe will breeze into my office about 11:35 looking harried and worn. He will cave into my chair and say, "My God, Urb! I've just got to get away from the pressure for a while. I haven't even had time this week to stop for lunch!" He will then go into a long story about the many things he has to do before the weekend—and in the process we will miss our lunch. And I will go home at 5:30 this afternoon and tell

Jeanette, "Gee, Honey, what a day! Didn't even stop for lunch!" Because I, too, am a past master at Busytell. Did anyone think for a moment that I was going to listen to all that stuff of Joe's without telling him how busy I was?

Pressure? We're all under tremendous pressure these days. A whole generation of psychiatrists and medical people have gotten rich telling us: "The world is moving too fast!" "We're all working too hard!" "Slow down and live!"

There is no question about the pressure. Men are dying of heart attacks all over the country, and at very early ages. Ulcers have become a status symbol.

American males consume billions of aspirin products and millions of tranquilizers each year. But where does the pressure come from? Do we really work that hard? Or is it, perhaps, that we are kidding ourselves? Could it be that the pressure is created because we are *not* doing enough real, honest work and we know it? In other words, are we that busy? Or do we waste too much time telling each other—and ourselves—how busy we are?

And there is another question that all of us need to ask as we search for real meaning in the word "masculine." Granted, we are busy; very busy. But *what* are we busy *at*? How important are most of the things we do? Do we do them because we *have* to? Or are we "keeping ourselves busy" because we are really secretly avoiding the things we hate to do, yet know have to be done?

Right now, I am busy—I am feeling a tremendous amount of pressure from two things on my desk. The first is a stack of unanswered correspondence. It has accumulated all week, and absolutely *must* go out today.

The second is this chapter. It has been sitting in front of me with a title on it for 30 days. It absolutely *must* go out today.

Both of these things were on my desk yesterday and the day before. Yet yesterday, I spent the entire afternoon "planning." I sat there squiggling figures on a piece of paper. A high-level "executive" has to spend a lot of time "just thinking," doesn't he? And the day before—two hours in a "conference" with Chuck Tooman. A half hour on the phone with Dick Ayres; 20 minutes with Vic Holliday. And all of the time this article and that correspondence were jangling the pressure-bell of my nerve-ends and shouting to my conscience, "We've got to be done; we've got to be done!"

It might be interesting, in our search for a genuine male mystique, to examine the "pressures" on an ordinary man in an ordinary day. Let's select a desk-bound man, because I am a desk-bound man. But if you, the people who are looking at yourselves with me, are sincere in your personal search, don't hesitate to substitute butcher, baker, factory worker. Here is how a long, tough, ten-hour day sometimes looks to me:

7:00 a.m. Rise. There are two primary ways of rising: (a) Sleep until the last minute and rush; (b) get up early and drink coffee and be unsociable and take time to get gathered for a hard day. Either system works well in avoiding your wife's questions about Johnny's dental appointment. ("Can we pay a little on the bill this time?") Or about talking to Suzie's teacher. ("You take care of that, honey; I don't have time to think about it now.") So two unanswered questions—the dental bill and Suzie's schoolwork—leave for the office with him and stay there as pressure.

7:45 a.m. Arrive at office—early, of course. This is a busy man. A hurried nod to the secretary—"many things to do; keep me undisturbed today."

7:50 a.m. A quick and businesslike look at the things on the desk. A report that is partly finished—that doesn't need to be done immediately. The day's correspondence; that can be delayed. An article for a magazine—that needs to be done now, but it's going to have to wait until he works himself into a "creative mood."

8:00 a.m. Walks to window to create creative mood. Looks out, sees children going to school. Wonders whether dentist will insist on a payment before he fixes Johnny's teeth. Starts uncharitable train of thought on dentists.

8:45 a.m. Still nothing on paper. "Too many things on my mind." Goes to discuss the article with Chuck. Chuck: "Glad you came in, Urb. I'm having trouble starting this morning. Look at this mess on my desk." Pressure—both need time off—fishing . . .

10:00 a.m. Return from fishing trip. Still not creative. Call secretary; examine financial report again. Worry about report.

10:30 a.m. Phone rings. Al. Coffee? You bet. Need to get out of this madhouse for a while. Fails to impress Al with busy; Al is even busier.

11:10 a.m. Article. Damn article. Get the correspondence out first.

11:50 a.m. Fifth letter requires considerable thought and some research.

Answer that later. Time for lunch; terrible morning. Where did the time go?

And so—4:30—clerical staff leaves. "Oh, poor me" time. Everybody goes home, I gotta work. Article half done; correspondence half done. Last look at financial statement. Still red.

5:00 p.m. To hell with it. Work tonight. Article in briefcase. Correspondence in briefcase. Greeting for wife and kids: "Just leave me alone for a while. Give a man a chance to unwind. Terrible day . . ."

And then the TV set. The cowboys . . . merciful, unthinking cowboys. Blocks out wife's glare; she still wants to talk about those teeth. Damn teeth. Women should be able to make those little decisions. Responsibility—have to talk to her about that. Pretty—she's pretty when she's mad. Home should be relaxing—loving—*will* talk to her about that—right after *Mission Impossible*—and one more drink . . .

So then the dawn, and a new day; one that starts with ulcer certainly and promises to move on to coronary possibility. Pressure. Dentist still there. Teacher. Article. Report. Correspondence. And a new dimension: wife who is mean and ugly because she thinks she has been used.

Busy? To hell with it, men. This book is

about honesty; about a real, genuine search for what manhood means.

"Busytell" is where it is at for a lot of us; probably most of us who operate under "tremendous pressure." Most of us don't need a vacation, or even a night out with the boys. We can relax any time by doing the things that need to be done.

Self-discipline is a word that needs to be revived in the 1970's; it needs to become again a part of the meaning of manhood. We all have things to do, and they need to be done—not for "other people's sake," but for our own peace of mind.

There was a time when discipline was immature; it came from the *outside*. Bosses were slave drivers who stood at our shoulders and forced us to do what needed to be done. But today, almost every man who works is in a seller's market. His labor union protects him; his boss can't spare him. With rare exceptions, no one tells him exactly what he must do and when he must do it. Society even supports him when he is lazy. He is laughed at and called a "company man" when he does too much.

Yet there is only *one* essential ingredient to a real male mystique. At the end of each day, a man has to look at himself and like what he sees. Other people are important, yes; but we only begin to be able to get along with other people when we learn to live with ourselves.

For most of us, there are two main areas of our lives in which we have to learn to live with ourselves, and they cannot be separated. The first is our job; the second is our home. A "hard day at the shop" can build hell at home, and a tension-filled home stays with us every minute of the working day.

As I grow older, every now and then I have a peaceful day. Without exception, these are the busy days; the days I do what needs to be done. On those nights I go home and Jeanette looks beautiful because I don't look so bad myself.

But then there are the Busytell days— still way too many of them. These are the nights that I go home and grouse and complain, drink a lot, and look for sympathy by telling everyone who will listen how tough it all is.

It doesn't make sense—but then we men seldom do. The little egos are far too weak to do what needs to be done—and then face our families with the quiet pride and confidence that make a loving home. Somehow we hang on to the hope that we will get the things that we need by *talking* about what we are doing, rather than by getting things done.

And yet, male pride and confidence—a sense of a job well done, a person created, or more love built—these are the things that manhood is all about.

# Chapter 8
# Genuine Men

And yet, I've been lucky enough to know a dozen genuine men in my lifetime. You know them, too, and that's the first remarkable thing about them; everyone recognizes them as thoroughly masculine.

Each of them has a "story." Some of their stories are long and involved, and a few of the chapters are not pretty. Yet failure, dishonesty, or even despair has not discouraged them from continuing the search for their real selves—and this, it seems, is what separates these men from the boys. They kept looking, kept searching until eventually they discovered who they were and what they stood for. In the process, they developed a sense of integrity, of personal worth. They can look at themselves and like what they see.

As I write this chapter, I think of Ed, a genuine man. Ed, a Unitarian, was 90 the last time I saw him. Perhaps Ed has passed on now, but I don't know why he should. At 90 he was sharp, useful, constructive, interested. He was in touch with people around him and he liked and respected them. It was easy for him, because somehow Ed had learned to like and respect himself.

I think often about life after death, and I wonder about it. As I think about Ed, I can see him sitting talking with his Unitarian Christ, chuckling and reminiscing. Both of them are grown-ups now, so they won't be spending much time feeling guilty or condemning people who seemed to stand in the way of their personal growth and maturity.

Ed could condemn, if he wanted to. There certainly was a father, or a mother, in his background who did everything possible to keep Ed from becoming what he was destined to become. All of us have that kind of mother or father at some time during our lives. Fathers and mothers are a part of their culture, their society. Without even thinking about it, they tend to divide their children's characters into "good" traits and "bad" traits. A parent's task: to stamp out the bad, encourage the good.

This immediately divides the person against himself. Sigmund Freud would say that we were suppressing the Id; Philip Wylie that we were setting the person in conflict with his instinct. As Christians, we can view this accepted parental process in still another way; arrogant human beings trying to alter the design of the person built into him by God.

Suppose, for example, that Ed's father and mother decided that anger was a "bad" thing, and had to be stamped out. If they had succeeded, what would they have done to Ed?

First of all, they would be condemning Ed to a lifetime of mediocrity, because every great man in the history of mankind has been an angry man. Patient, kindly old John XXIII—with his anger toward people using Christ as an excuse for hating other Christians. Abraham Lincoln—humorous, understanding—and a violent anger for a system of slavery. Martin Luther King—and his hatred of racism. Christ, "meek and humble of heart"—and his anger at the Pharisees and the hypocrisy they stood for.

Even if his parents had only partially succeeded in stamping out Ed's anger, they would have created in him a constant tension; an internal war between what he is and what he has been told he should be. And Ed would never have been able to function as a man until he faced that tension.

Perhaps Ed's thing—the thing that *he* needed to face—was his anger.

Another genuine man that I know is quite a storyteller. He exaggerates outrageously and, as a result, he is an extremely interesting person to listen to. Besides, as a priest, he has an important message to sell, and this is how he sells it. He is well aware of his exaggerations, and he is not a bit disturbed about them. He knows that this is *Him;* and he likes what Him is able to accomplish.

This man, too, could spend a lot of time condemning people for trying to shape him into something that he was not. It does not take much of an imagination to recognize the struggle he went through before he became a "comfortable bunk-spreader." How many times, do you think, had someone called him a "liar"? How many times had his parents punished him for his "falsehood"?

And yet here he is today, one of the most effective teachers of Christianity that I know. Young people love to listen to him. They chuckle at his hilarious overstatements —and he chuckles with them. When they have laughed together, they become friends, and then they explore the real meaning of Christian. He is human, and he is not a bit afraid to show them his humanity. So they can talk with him.

Twelve of them. Twelve genuine men, out of the many men that I know. Their "story" separates them from the Real Men— the phony-baloneys—and the rest of us who are slowly traveling someplace between Real and Genuine. They stand out and are recognized in any crowd. And yet this story of theirs is relatively simple.

It started with a decision made sometime not to be anyone's "boy"; not Mother's or Dad's or society's, or even his wife's. But somehow, to find themselves, and then be.

The genuine men that I know are neither conformists nor nonconformists. Instead, they are uniquely themselves. They are secure enough in what they are so that they do not have to worry much about what other people think of them. They have found themselves, and that is the most important discovery that any man can make.

But although their stories are simple, the living of them has not been simple. Like all of us, they started out their adulthood as "Real Men" with all of the fears, dishonesties, and pretensions that are common to all of us.

The difference between them and the rest of us is that most of us continue to live with our fears, dishonesties and pretensions, because it seems to be easier. *We want people to like us so desperately that we are willing to live with any kind of facade which we think will protect us from being hurt.*

But it's *not* easier to live that way. The things that are in us—the things built into us by a loving Creator—have to come out in useful constructive ways—or they will stay inside and fester or explode and kill us as effective people.

No one gets to know himself without considerable pain. A person who has been taught from infancy that half of what he is is "good" and the other half is "bad" can never look at all of him in perfect comfort.

Yet all of the genuine men that I know have taken this look. And they keep taking it every day. And slowly they have come to see that the things they are are not good or bad, but just "things" put there by a loving Creator to be used in a constructive or a destructive way.

All of my genuine men are sometimes impatient. One has ulcers. Another drinks quite a bit. Still a third can be an absolute bore when he starts to talk about his hobby.

Yet all of them have quite a few things in common, too. It's the common traits—the ones that seem to be shared by every genuine man—that we will want to explore in our final chapter.

# Chapter 9
# A Better Definition
# of Masculinity

*The Male Mystique* is drawing to a close and
I find myself dissatisfied with it. Writing it
has been good for me; it has intensified my
personal search for the meaning of
masculinity. And yet, in this final chapter,
I still find myself with a hundred questions
to ask. Are the twelve I mentioned in the
last chapter really genuine men? Or do they
simply fit nicely into my own definition of
genuine? Do I think they are great because
they are a little like me? Aren't most men
genuine in some respects and totally phony
in others? What *would* happen to the world
if we suddenly became totally honest?

Maybe a genuine man is a complete

phony—who spends all of his lifetime becoming a little less phony. And a "Real Man" may be one who goes through his entire life not even knowing he is a phony.

And yet, in all of this personal confusion, there is a little logic. There are some things we can work on; some characteristics that we know are completely masculine. We have a model: the One Man among us who succeeded in achieving true masculinity. What can we learn from his life?

He was patient, meek, gentle, kind, long-suffering, charitable. These things we know; they have been drummed into us from childhood. But that is just a tiny part of the picture. We accept these things as part of the attributes of Christianity, and I think that most of us do try to work on them.

But if these characteristics were all of Christ, then he certainly wouldn't be much of a model of masculinity. These characteristics also describe the night crawler that I use on my fishing trips. This worm is patient, loving, long-suffering, gentle—and so charitable that he will sacrifice his life for my enjoyment. If this were all that there were to Jesus, I would treat him, I'm afraid, like a worm. I wouldn't think about him at all—except when I needed a far-out and somewhat shocking analogy for an article. Fortunately, I just don't see Jesus on a fishhook. Fortunately, too, I don't see him *only* on a cross.

Instead I see him walking proudly through life, glad that he is who he is and never hesitating to tell anyone what he believes in. I see him telling people that he is Christ, the Son of God, and this is what he was born to be.

I think this is something we can do. Someplace, in the mess of talents we have been given, we can discover that which we were born to be. And then we can forget about social climbing and what the neighbors think and even how much money it brings in and *be* that thing, in pride and increasing confidence. It seems to me there is a lot of measuring in the words, "God created us," because they imply God created us *for some reason*. Why spend time doing things ineffectively? Why fight ourselves— and fight God? Why not find out who we are, and what we do well, and then do that thing with confidence in ourselves *and* in God?

Something tells me that we might even make money if we do.

Christ didn't just walk proudly; he walked honestly. In all of his life, we do not see a single example of hypocrisy. He never bothered to be better than he was, or different, or even more humble. He hated hypocrites. Prostitutes, crooks, extortionists, even murderers—all were met with some understanding. But not the phonies. They received the full benefit of his anger. "Woe to you, scribes and Pharisees, hypocrites!" These terrible words make me shudder when I am playing my phony little masculine game.

So this is something concrete that we can do, too. We can work on our little hypocrisies, search them out, try to eliminate them. And we can take a risk now and then by refusing to go along with other people's little games. With each small victory over hypocrisy, it becomes a little easier to look at ourselves and like what we see. Self-love, integrity, personal dignity, self-respect; whatever name you give it, Christ had plenty of it. He knew who he was, and he liked what he was. He had his work to do and that work was important. He wasn't driven by guilt to respond to every human call for help. He would have made a great king, but that was not what he was there for. So he turned it down. He could have spent all his days and nights in counseling people, driving on until he fell in complete exhaustion. He could have come

on a fast horse, or a cloud, if necessary,
scattering the seeds of Christianity thinly
and erratically over thousands of miles and
many different peoples. But he didn't.
Instead, he stayed with his small group, and
did what he could do best. He built solidly,
slowly and well. He traveled on a donkey,
or walked; gave himself plenty of time to
think things through. He knew his assets,
but also knew his limitations. And he
respected those limitations because he liked
himself. Once in a while he went up in the
mountains to get away from people. Or took
a boat ride. All with no apologies.

In other words, Christ knew how to say
*No*. One can imagine him being a Little
League coach, or a PTA president, or
Knights of Columbus member, or a worker
in the ghettoes, or a contributor to the Red
Cross, or a member of the church choir, or
even the secretary of a bowling league. But
it is impossible to imagine him as *all* of
these things.

But many of us try to be all of these
things and many more; father, husband,
pastor. Some of us do it for attention. Many
more of us are driven by guilt. We believe
the crusaders—and the nuts—who tell us
that we are responsible for race prejudice,
juvenile delinquency, drugs, crime in the

streets, bad breath, and the failure of the parish fund drive. So we spread ourselves thin and do nothing much in many places, and then, in discouragement, we do nothing at all.

All because of a lack of self-respect, a sense of personal worth. So this, too, is something positive that we can do to become genuine men. We can recognize that we have some limitations. The world can stand only one God at a time. We can learn to respect those limitations, concentrate on our strengths, and so again, learn to look at ourselves and like what we see.

Finally, when we learn to love ourselves, we can again do a better job of loving others. Jesus, the Eternal Do-Gooder; let's get rid of him. He's not for real. Because he respected himself, he also respected others. He loved them. Didn't worry about always being "nice" to them. Cared enough for Peter to point out he was a braggart. Cared enough about the Pharisees to show them what they were. With all of the power at his command, he still didn't try to force his apostles into a mold; didn't try to make them carbon copies of himself. Instead, he respected them, accepted them, continued to talk with them until they found courage, identity, faith.

This also we can do to become a little more masculine. We can respect people, accept them, care enough about them to be honest with them.

Courage, honesty, a sense of personal worth, introspection, humor, respect for other people, love for them, mature caring: These are some of the elements of masculinity we have been exploring in our search for a genuine male mystique.

And here, in summary, is my problem with this book. Here is the reason I've had so much trouble writing it. Here is the reason I almost abandoned it; felt that the book itself was phony.

Because aren't all of these qualities we have talked about the characteristics of a *genuine woman,* too?